Sixty Years
of
Loving

'... may my feet follow my wider glance
First no doubt to stumble – then to walk with the others
And in the end – with time and luck – to dance'
Louis MacNeice, **Autumn Journal**

'She is a Creole girl and she have the sun in her'
Jean Rhys, **Wide Sargasso Sea**

Sixty Years of Loving

Maggie Harris

Cane Arrow Press

First published 2014 by
Cane Arrow Press
PO Box 219
Royston
SG8 1AZ

British Library Cataloguing in Publication Data.
A catalogue record for this book is available from the British
Library

ISBN 978-0-9562901-7-5

Cover drawing by Maggie Harris

Guyanese-born Maggie Harris now lives in Wales and her work has always emerged from a collision of cultures. Her poetry locates itself at the meeting place of West Indian memory and a British context and reinforces the good things about hybrid existence. For Maggie, the meeting place of cultures is often a site of myth making and metamorphosis.

Love, sexual attraction, youth, poignancy and humour are only some of the emotions present in this collection, defined by that migrant voice that continues to move between the Caribbean and Britain.

Maggie Harris's sixth collection of poetry coincides with and celebrates her sixtieth birthday through poetry centred on a love of language, individual narratives and voice. It draws inspiration from musicians and poets including Leonard Cohen and Derek Walcott, its perspective spanning time and place.

A former Guyana Prizewinner, Maggie's other works include *Kiskadee Girl,* a memoir, and *Canterbury Tales on a Cockcrow Morning,* a book of short stories inspired by Chaucer and modern life.

For my family and friends whose love and encouragement has been manna for the soul, and for those whose words and music gave me wings.

CONTENTS

Stop All the Clocks

Time is racing ahead of me in the heat
Wearing yellow cotton with scattered parakeets
Her palm is outstretched, the gold on her wrists
Harnessing the Sun God, that destroyer of men,
The life-blood of Cane.
In the gloom of the market-place her pale skin bleeds
Through yesterday's harvest – sapodillas and bora beans,
Bales of Indian cotton, knuckle-bones, bloodied cow heels.
The butcher's hands are swift, his tone accommodating
To the Captain's wife whose small child hides in the folds
Of a parakeet's wing.
Dung and dust, fish-heads, bones.
Beyond red mullet and hassa's black primeval scales,
Open ground: the sun firing pyramids of peppers
Molten mounds of melons, black-skinned babies asleep
Under parasols, the gold on their mothers' arms alight
Palms cupping coppers, musical notes fed by the river breeze
Ushered by that Atlantic hanging on the Canje horizon
The cries of the insane circling
Like swifts.

Stop all the clocks.

The cliffs are as white as they sing, with castles and ramparts
Martello towers, smugglers haunts. At Margate, Eliot
and Walcott watched the sea; Englishness and poetry
Loud as the parakeets settling in Kentish trees. And time
Is a jester on a train, cheery as he cuts through flat fields
Of lavender and rape; hop-poles like stiltmen at Sittingbourne

Stunted apples at Ash, Pick-Your- Own at Cliffsend
Children's mouths full of strawberries;
Flans, shortcake, a grand-parents' garden, wisteria and roses.
And out of the dark earth the Morris Men dance;
Blackened faces holding torches high above the crowd
Marching like an army down to Broadstairs harbour, the dragon
Beside them wild, as Jonkannu. But those lining the streets
Are only half-aware of Folk; from small gatherings in the park
Where country dancers clog-hop on wooden boards, decades
Spin to neon, Arts Council Grants, *Elf and Safely*;
Marquees, licensing laws releasing the need to get as pissed
As possible. Now copulating thousands have culled this ritual
Of fire, the flames setting out to sea
Like a funeral pyre.

Stop all the clocks.

Red kites swoop and screech above Tregaron.
There are no parakeets here. The dragon flies
His banner red and bold; slayers come weekly
Property brochures in hand. But *he*
Is re-born each year in Newcastle Emlyn;
The fight to free the Welsh tongue, loosen the reins
From the English, firing his dragon's breath in
Every town and valley.
Walcott's *Far Cry to Africa* is unknown to Somalians
Fleeing those shores so many West Indians dreamed
Was the real Mother Country. Still, synonyms remain.
The singing of rivers reaming below each tarmacked road
The black rocks of Pembrokeshire breaking their teeth
On the angry Irish sea; the peaks of mountains

Disappearing into the mist. Pink ribbons fade on the gateposts
Of Machynlleth. Time is the uncurl of a peony bud
The random splatter of Welsh poppies, the raised faces
Of Michaelmas daisies to a grudging sun.
It is my mother at the garden gate
Inching her way down the stones.

Stop all the clocks.

Elizabeth

I'm calling her name as I fall
head first through the window
Elizabeth. She is the one
whose skirts enfold me like sails
rubs mud from my wrists
curls my hair with a wet comb.
She is the lady in blue
singing hymns and Doris Day
carving kiss-curls on her cheekbones.
Later she will untangle my arms
from her pleated waist
leaving her lips on my wet face
and step out into the sun
carried on a perfumed mist
into a cloud of crotons and roses.

Sisters

As grown women now, cruising Debenhams, eyes out
for bargains, remembering how skinny we were all once
our girl-hearts trilling like birds
who amongst us sees the market-place, rows upon rows
of fibre and plastic, leather and lace, with price tags
unrelated to anything real? We are macaws and kiskadees
who sang *Sweet Sacrament Divine*
dressed in georgette in another life. There trade
and commerce forged an alliance which brought us into being.
No wonder then my feet ache along endless aisles of
merchandise
and I reach for the memory of us playing in the back yard
with stones, twigs, and a calabash.

Coming up for Thirteen

coming up for 13 and the promise of morning
ablaze like the sun on the front porch
anointing the banisters, inviting the descent
into the yard in seersucker shorts and toenails
of bougainvillea

the pedals of the Moulton bike wait in the shadows
of the bottom-house, watch the dismissive curl
of her lip as younger sisters jump hopscotch
on hot concrete, their home-made skirt-tails flying
and the minutes are so long

hanging in the guava tree in air heavy with bird-beat wings
the boy suspended on the telegraph pole
children's tow-heads caught like stars
in the frame of the lasso –
skipping-rope risen into the blue sky

beyond them the posse – teenage friends
in the street
the chorus of bicycle bells

Through Blue Eyes to Mali
(For Salif Keita)

I heard they sliced the fingers of musicians
and the tongues of singers
if there was a moment when the world changed, it was then.

That beautiful woman on tv
bringing Mali's open wounds to bleed
on hard-backed chairs... you might well break a linnet
tear its limbs and feathers from its fragile throat.

Africa, I am a Caribbean child
my father bore your music in his bones
and shared it on verandas
when the day was done

right through Billy Graham and Elvis
Demerara windows, housewives rocking, men lazing on
plantation chairs, woven and stripped
from the backs of men.

Picking tunes
from gospel
through to river blues -
his grey eyes watched a shifting world
that bore him blue-eyed daughters. If he knew
a song of Africa
he didn't say.

Those guitar strings bled blues too deep to dwell on;

bodies settled for perching, the long end of days.

But in all the choirs I ever sung
and all the incense swung
in all the Latin litanies
and Pentecostal tongues
no fire burned as wildly
as that winter afternoon
a song from Mali
found me
where these feet had led me
where the winds had blown me

Babel
where I swept the table bare
of sacraments and testaments
and things which didn't fit

I was not to know
I was preparing;
that calabash bowls that bathed us
from that river running red
were living gourds
in Africa's forgotten earth

> *O Fathers, you anointed me*
> *With waters from the wells*
> *You stumbled through the cities*
> *Of the Bells*
> *All the time believing those stories that you told*
> *Were everlasting truth, and nothing but the truth*

And with those lies you stole away my youth...

But somehow sonic passages
still reverberated
a caravanserai of longing
rode the marrow
in my father's broken bones
his finger on guitar strings
echoed the prologue
of a past he didn't know
and when that voice from Mali came
I didn't know the words
but recognised the tune
the
honey
pouring
on my splintered soul
the longing

and these words, these words I write
I score them on the page and know
if 400 years of dying
could not rip out a heart
no knife will slice the voice
no knife will slice the voice
the songs will find a rhythm all their own

I Wanted to Remember Him Young

I wanted to remember him young
bare-skinned on the hammock
watching me through narrowed eyes

nights then were black as sin
heavy with congregations of crickets
a nun's glide on a thin corridor of light

those brief hours
the river silent alongside
a dying night of wood-smoke
hurried by the approach of dawn
my blue Timex watch ticking
my mother's rosary beads
crossing Main St

and all my body wanted
was to be kissed
and kissed
whilst I died in his arms

I wanted to remember him young
he was a God then
and died
time gobbled him up
stole him.
I was young;
Oh yes, I was young.

This Morning We Were a Picasso

This morning we were a Picasso
legs bronze cylinders
hair daubed on a pillow of alizarin crimson

your cheekbones were geometric planes
your Roman breasts
discs of gold, small chariots wheeling on runnels

of blood and dust.
The morning sun splintered the coins
of our navels; neat half-moons

dreaming of re-entering eternity.

This morning we were Picassos
right angled hues
    -    Except for your precious eyes
They were jewels. Van Goghs. A sea of pupils.

Stigmata Rock

His passion bends his body like a wave
folding his guitar into the cave
of his chest, stretching his fingers
like strings, raw catgut
twisted fishing lines
caught in Neil Young's *Like a Hurricane.*

It is a trapped eel, flailing
to be free, to be flung
on a shore where there is peace
away from this ecstasy of pain
that's entered its incongruous Magritte-self
into this back room pub littered
with the casings of the soul -
a sea bed of guitars and amplifiers
octopi wires looping
whilst he the Navigator
beneath the spool of light
is barely aware of the circle of eyes
or the hush that descends
or the blood that streams
corpuscular red between the reels of his fingers.

When All the Music's Played

When all the music's played
and the crowds have gone
here in my skin and bone
are left these broken songs

They're homeless on the highway
strangers on the road
seeking friends of blackbirds and
staring at the moon

They've travelled far from mornings
cut right through the pain
praying for someone to whistle up
some   kind of tune

Bring me banjos, folk guitars
harmonicas and flutes
violins and mandolins
I can't go on alone

The traveller alone is
a traveller unknown
and broken songs are poems
seeking flesh and bone.

For Leonard Cohen

I cannot say I love you
in the way women love, or men.
I am no hard-fast fan who
would besiege you with roses or emails
and vow to hold you to my breast
to fill the hole my soul seeks.
No. Let me make it clear
I do not mean to walk in your footsteps
some artificial shadow
stealing words from your sleeves or
dreaming of a time we could have shared
in Greece where I would be your Marianne
the Martha in the harem.
No. I love you for the way you
opened my heart and mind by braving
the abyss; to allow myself to fall, to fail,
to face the grip that testaments and
sacraments had bound my spirit tight
in fear and breathlessness.
I love you for the introduction:
to raise the beauty, rescue the poetry
from Genesis, permit desire to occupy a place
walk the harbour wall.
This is love too –
walking on the water, smoke and mirrors,
Samson's hair falling. Hallelujahs.

Even As I Sleep

Even as I sleep the mountains sing
I have not yet had my fill
The trees like windswept soldiers
Brace their march against the hill

They sing against my blue-veined skin
With throats of bark and honeyed wood
And fill my ear like promises
Like hymns.

Saartje's Song

If I could sing I would sing you a song
Of the taste of salt past Madagascar

On the Cornish coast
grows tremendous wild a fig,
the *Hottentot.*

So too, they called us,
convoluted our tongue
re-christening each stone and clod of earth
naming.

From oceans far they sang of it
came in their hundreds with pickaxe and Bible
book and prod, charcoal and paint
rope and ink, mapping.

This tale you will not find in libraries
but in signs
carried on the wind
in cargo holds, the empiricism of men.

One can no longer imagine
weeks and months of sail, the struggle of
the mouth to describe such wonderful fanciful things
they christened *strange*

if I could sing I would sing you a song
of the taste of salt past Madagascar

the coal and soot of London town
the wolves of men whose eyes burned the circle round me;
France, and men who journeyed my body
with pen, paint, penis.

Now I am a glory be, home they said.
But, on the Cornish coast grows wild and glorious
 a fig, The Hottentot.
It is hard to contain, I believe.

*Inspired by the story of Saartjie Baartman, a Khoikhoi woman
exhibited as a freak show attraction in 19th C Europe. 'Hottentot' is
now considered an offensive term.*

How Do I Love You?

(With a nod to EBB)

How do I love you?
Let me count the ways –
Your picture's on my bedroom wall
Your socks are on the chaise

How do i love you?
Let me count the ways
I love you for your stubble
I love you for your gaze

Your name falls always from my lips
My mind is in a daze
I fold your likeness in the sheets
My origami phase

How i **do** love you!
With the sun's glare and the wind's strength
The lifeboat's launch and the rain's torrent
With a cat's soft paws and a tiger's chase
And the whoosh of a bar-b-q's flare
With the last ferrero and a courtesan's stare
I loved you so
And i love you still.

For an Afghan Woman Poet

Nadia, Nadia. I will repeat your name
to break like waves, a tidal refrain
washing again and again in the wake
of your silenced tongue.
Laugh at the morning, you wrote,
shut the door on the night;
words of hope that cradled
your fear of a place called home
where the blow that felled you like a tree
still flies free.
You were a warrior,
fighting with fists of verbs
etching your right to life
on stolen scraps of paper
the book open at the kitchen table
whilst you stirred the pot
and held your small son's smile.
Nadia. Between us lie continents,
deserts of imagined worlds woven,
spun from dry winds, dust and stones
of a land men stalk.
But even as the heads of the Buddhas roll
their sacred dust implodes, becomes the air
they breathe.
Nadia, you will never be silenced. Names and words are
long forgotten whilst yours rises still,
sing like kites.

Sea Water

Sea water, I was told, will not assist the act of love*
So I chose me a waterfall
And seven miles of rain
I caught a conch to call you by
And installed a weather vane

Sea water, I was told, will not assist the act of love
So I scrubbed salt water from my skin
And moisturised my scales
Investigated boreholes
And below-ground limestone caves

My seasons ushered monsoons
I scuttled whole lagoons
To sift crustaceans from a sand
That dared reflect a moon

But lovers came and went, none stayed,
And only now I know
 the significance of my name
Running Water, Foot-first Child, Forest Rain.

*Quote from a poem by Richard Gwyn

They Say That on Warm Nights

They say that on warm nights:
They swim and tumble
On the turning tides, and loll like sirens
Full-blown and laughing
Young girls at play

They say that just as young girls
Cannot contain themselves
They rise as one tide, a choral wave
Rushing to embrace dry land
And us, curious, brave
Until, like us
They come face to face with fear

The Day the Sun Came Out

The day the sun came out
she went knicker-less
in a sun-dress plucked from the back of her wardrobe –
blue calico with sheen of peacock

The house breathed open, windows yawned
poppies ranted from back-o-yard
bearded irises hummed
the geraniums burst into O Sole Mio
Hip-hop climbed the vine
the ivy rhymed

By the runner beans
her bare toes caught on a stone
the message shooting up along her thigh
trumpeting a wild plea she ignored
preferring to remember his mouth
drinking from her like a fountain
hearing for the first time
how the ground roared

We Buried Them Together

We buried them together
up the slope by the summer-house
where on warm days we would sit
with coffee or with wine

one and then the other
would follow, a languorous walk
upwards: pausing to sniff a fallen
branch or invader's scent

then content to sit
in the shade or spring on our lap
with the memory of youth
. claws coming to grief on fabric

It was a good day for renewal
New Year's Day 2013
and we toasted them with Christmas Baileys
-    Lidl's best.

A Moment with Gauguin, Tate Modern

No one mentions the Martinique women.

Colour erupts; desire exploding red and raw
slash of breast, leaf, arm, cheek
beaten out from canvas like pheasants.

Words - *Myth, him, Eden,*
Tahiti - fall from learned lips
 with so much longing they resound
around these catacombs
of fallen fruit and
women bleeding landscape
through guarded eyes and luscious skin

all dead now
that gold pawpaw skin
this crowd beneath the 19th C brochures,
liners and palms
all ash beneath the Polynesian sun.

Ghosts stumble out into the gift-shop, eyes
like missionaries.
From the balcony, St Paul's hoards the horizon.
No-one mentions the Martinique women.

You are No Bruce Willis

You are no Bruce Willis
I think this as we share tea and biscuits
and you watch the birds through the glass
dancing their fandangle thing
by the nuts.
You're dressed for winter
   -    not a good look –
woolly hat still on from when
you walked the dog
and your fingers are knuckled and raw
not from punching terrorists
or swinging from tower blocks
but from wrestling the cold
and cutting logs with a hand-saw.

I'd be lying if I said I wouldn't
fancy a tussle with Bruce (Die Hard 1)
all sweat and muscle –
though not on my nicely made-up bed
with the Egyptian cotton from Debenhams;
maybe the dining table
where you laboured long and hard
with the sanding.

Anyway, who really wants to die hard
when you could live soft
and I always did like the touch of your hands.

Homelands

My mother's altar has migrated
travelled uncomplainingly in a Madeira trunk
once bound from the Azores to the Indies
sailed past the island of Goree where my father's bones
had waited, shackled by marrow and Ashanti prayers.

In the New World, a Cathedral of sugarcane
stretched above the fields, knees
bend in the heat and mud learning
about hosannas at noon;
from a gully, a half-remembered tune

whittled from home-grown flutes.

1950s. A home-made altar.
timbers stippled with wood-ants
a crucifix on the wall, Christ nailed;
beside him Good Friday palms,
the yard flowers, his American portrait
Christ Knocking at the Door.

The Madeira trunk sits beneath the window
taking in the breeze, the smell
of ground masala, smoking cane fields
the sound of children growing.
He remembers the Atlantic. Inside him
Portuguese linen, folded, stiff with starch,
a wedding veil.

We spoke in tongues; splintered Latin and Creole
torn from Gods, dismembered.
Yemaya, Mary, Jesu Christo. Obeah men
slit roosters' throats and danced till whips gave way
to bicycles to motorcars on streets with English names
in Dutch towns, *Nieuw Amsterdam, koker dams, Paramaribo*...

2010. Altar, Southeast England,
screws from Homebase
Apostles, Our Lady's blue smile, her son's bleeding heart
postcards of Wells Cathedral
scented candles from the Garden Centre.

Wales 2013. The Madeira trunk sits waiting
for its cracking skin of splintered oak and tin
to be distressed to shabby chic
its pewter fixings breaking free of mustard yellow paint
brushed by my grand-mother's young hands
filled with linen, rosaries, hope.
Now, in its dark belly hold – a new cargo –
old photographs and books, certificates
my Mother's hair from 1956,
bridesmaids dresses –
hold their breath, remembering

those other passages
Atlantic waters, souls
cheek by jowl, bone to soul.

He sits beneath the window listening
to the ceaseless song

a Welsh river running
the rhythm of the wind in the trees
there are footsteps on the gravel,
laughter,
Bora Da

Cleopatra Herself in All her Glory

Cleopatra herself in all her glory
couldn't look as good I did
done up in all my finery
for an assignation with you.
Maybe I was in denial
but there's something about an affair
that apart from feeling horny
makes you Queen-like
and so beautiful you love yourself just looking.
The noise your skin makes shining
drowns out the crickets
rivals the fireflies
goes out into the world singing
like a pissed fly and if coconuts
fell on your head you wouldn't notice
just keep on walking with that stupid smile on your face
and a heart banging away like a djembe.
I'm dreaming here, wondering
which lover am I thinking about
was it the one who met me at the station
with the bike, knowing
I'd mentioned how much I'd liked
riding on the crossbar, my head
tucked in nicely against the chest
of some Old Spiced boy?
It could even be the hots I got
for a goddess once, driving along
some moon-lit road
but that couldn't last, that was some

different kind of loving
and I'm nothing without my lippy.
Or it could be you, my current bun
my liver-spotted Die Hard 10
the lover for whom my beauty ripened
like a pomegranate, and all the ugly bits
I'd covered up matured all of a sudden
like vines ripened on the Bosporus.
Cleo, you had nothing on me then.

Remembering Star-apples

Remembering star-apples
And the moment you slice them – the star
The melt on your tongue, the black seed?
O Lord I have forgotten ... the skin black?
Flesh purple? 1960 something ...

Here, I am an apple, eat me
A Satsuma, a grape, a cherry
I stand before you, heart undone
Bleached by a post-colonial sun
Barefoot, a nomad reading orchids
The split between lip and cheek

... there I am on the front step
My teeth splitting star-apples.
That I remember.

October Harvest

The Aunts are dying;
one by one in Northern countries they are falling,
a late crop that had held on to their shoots
like Civil War women,
uprooted aging bones and flesh
to escape small revolutions, racial and economic disparity.

They leave this earth with the smell of camphor balls
and Limacol, with memories of secret gins
and servant girls learning to take orders
from newly married 'coloured' women
to sugar's October harvest.

I remember them like polished fruit,
glass apples on a Bookers' dining table
reflected on the greenheart floor where I, the country child
tiptoed past my cousins' bedrooms,
gleaming caves of comic books and records
straight from the US of A.

Aunt Leigh with the smile that surpassed
a thousand mistresses,
Aunt Joy, whose scissors shaped the futures
of three decades of uncut women,
several of whom caught her husband's eye,
or got the bank clerk job
or flew out on the arms of Toronto salesmen.

When it came their turn they left the guava

and the bougainvillea,
followed sons and daughters,
placed their tired feet on tired soil,
folded their fluttering hearts like envelopes
their souls in winter coats
stepped back five decades
into white countries that labelled them black.

The news comes in letters,
messages of memories and bodies fading,
my mother on the telephone,
her death-tone still,
preparing me for yet another
trans-Atlantic kill.

Nothing Nobody Tells You

Nothing nobody tells you will prepare you.
There she was, pint-sized and perfect
with alabaster skin and black gypsy curls
and the first thing I did was blub
for nothing I had ever done
in my small unimportant life
had ever ever ever
prepared me.

Photosynthesis

There they are, my three
freeze-framed in the doorway
spick and span, teeth cleaned
school-bags, lunch-boxes ready.
The shouting's done, the peeling out of bed
like caterpillars, the forcing down of Weetabix
the finding of tights, *no not the party ones*
the tears at hair-brushing, the rushing
to find a tin of something
for Harvest Festival.
I've locked this image in my mind
my magic three, my beautiful girls
my blue-eyed bouncing ballerinas
my screeching budgerigars;
no longer with me now
but out there in the world
making cakes and babies and careers
building their own memories
of multiplicative bliss,
light years of love, dimensions unquantifiable
as infinitesimal
as these pixels, these dancing jewels of atoms
their light heads against the doorway
shining.

Our Lady of the Harbour

Rain me fishes, *she cries*
small silverine things
with their eyes turned up to the sun
and their agile fins dancing
against the tresses of my hair;
I pin them to my crown
and become Lady Liberty.

They may struggle like the ripples
they made to Staten Island
thrash like fallen heads of corn
scythed in New England;
but I mind not:
suffering and gleaning
is all the same to me.

I hear they saw my mother
in the City of the Bells
head up laughing through the shopping malls
black hairs sprouting from her chin
still wearing the 50s bouffant frock
and smelling of cardamoms
and gin.
She was laughing all the while
I squatted at the mouth
of the Demerary pissing
and filtering the passages
of iron at Cardiff Bay
and yes, it was me

left my skin

on the rocks of Folkestone Harbour
where the children play
in the slippery promise of boats
anchors angling away
into memory of steamships
sailing past
those white cliffs of glory.

And now rich men have cometh
forth, built fountains
on the wharf-side there
-    Such a carnival! Ice-cream and beer –
and no-one notices me
waltz amongst them
watching their children

whose temporary laughter
rises
through
those
orchestrated
steepled
bullets of rain.

18

(For Aimee)

18 birthday balloons swing above the table
Where young girls toss their manes
Form a gable-end of foreheads
Jewelled arms and elbows, whispering.
Their laughter, light, loud,
Rises in the champagne air.
Downwind, low-bosomed matriarchs huddle
Frowns tight as the creases on their blouses
Wishing the evening would hurry up
And finish, not daring to remember
The thrill of it – that backless dress
Those killer heels stepping out
Into a breathless yet-to-be-discovered
Killer night.

When Someone Young

You think it, don't you, when someone young dies
You wonder why the fates have chosen them.
That young boy, barely fourteen
Falling to his death, the Facebook 'likes'
5000 in a day. So easy to think of analogies,
Icarus, or angels falling.
His cherubic face is smiling
A photo taken just the week before.
And you remember his mother
Whose own brother died, aged 18
Equally cherubic; and there they are now
Mother and daughter, grieving the death of sons.
And we think of all the evil men
Walking this earth, who live on and on and on
Battering their fists in the angled faces of women
And walking the road cock-a-hoop.
If you had a gun you would kill them all yourself
As if their absence would restore the presence
of the innocent and good.
But anger is a futile rider. Shock absorbs us
Catch us as we fall.
The brutal truth: *in the midst of life, in the midst of life...*
In the midst of life there is death.

Chillenden

Outlined against the skyline, blue t-shirt, hair scraped back
Tall golden corn...
We had scythed our way through calm countryside
Flat fields raked with ditches
Poppies on the banks
Stiles low enough for our daughter to clamber
Green black-berries, skewiff hedges;
In the distance, the windmill.
This is where they found them, hacked
Beneath a tree, mother, daughter, dog too.
I hide the photo. Can never return.

Watching Jeremy Kyle

Watching Jeremy Kyle
the bat and ball of words
like missiles, cannonballs
catapults, bows and arrows
rocket launchers
upsetting the sofa
bodies leaning forward, fingers pointing
dramatic entrances and exits backstage
cameras following
the stage an amphitheatre, roaring
for the lions to be let in
DNA tests, addicts
alcoholic fathers, grudges;
and underneath it all
the only thing that's missing
the only thing it's all about
that other four-letter word
they hardly ever use.

My Daughter, Age Sixteen

(For Angie)

My daughter, age sixteen, bought me a tree
And walked from Ramsgate to Broadstairs
Her Pre-Raphaelite face between its branches
Bearing me a birthday.
And I wondered at her beauty, brave
To wear a coronet of leaves
Through urban streets where anyone from school
Might have seen her. And I remembered
That Christingel when the candles nearly
Burnt her hair and the way she entered
Pre-school at the age of four, no tears, no looking back.
To open your front door and see
Your daughter's lovely face shining
Through a sea of green, and all their limbs
Still growing, was better than any birthday cake
And what a moment we shared, planting it.

I Remember You Well in the Chelsea Hotel

I remember you well in the Chelsea Hotel
No not really, Maidstone car park
sandwiches in the rain
Newcastle Emlyn, CK's sausage rolls hot
and that time you brought a treat
a chicken curry pasty.
There was a hotel once
St Lucia, uh huh
but I ain't talking 'bout that.

She's Seventy-six But Still Remembers

She's seventy six but still remembers
giggling like a girl
and then despair, he never came to find her
in the West.
I don't like to tell her he was doing what
such men did best
conquering brown skinned women
and promising them the world
forgetting it was never theirs to give.

Those Moments

Those moments –
a stranger locking eyes with you
across the bar, or a train pulling out
and you're in a spin, full tilt
galaxies are hurtling past the sandwiches
and you in a Matalan jacket not ostrich.

Slave Bangle, Wales

In tough times, only two things rise -
hope, and the price of gold,
ushered like hymns from the tavern
full-blown with the potential of proverbs
enter the cavern of the pawnshop;
third-world lives on first-world footsteps -
leather, crepe-soles, brogues -
bringing their barter to the goblin-men
before bailiffs come to the door.

The boy with the restless eyes
hip-hop on his mobile phone,
his grand-dad's medals warm
on his hipbone,

the widow in the sheepskin coat
squaring her shoulders to the task
of freeing her husband's watch
from its Victorian clasp;

and the brown-skinned woman-
accent weaving assonance
pawn to *porn*
unfolding tissue
lifted from a handbag littered
with council tax
and telephone
and central heating
bills.

She's been in a cavern before, in 1954;
a metal-tasting darkness
with flames on a far-back wall
where her child-eyes took to the light
and a Rumpelstiltskin spinning
St Christophers
out of molten gold.

He'd hammered a pattern of sugar-cane leaves
onto a ribbon of gold
curled it, wrapped it
around her mother's bones.

Now a Caribbean songbird breaks its beak against her throat
as another goblin weighs
in his cracked and calloused palm,
her slave bangle.
£9 for a gram -
the price of a bag of coal.

Meeting Rich People

Meeting rich people who used
to run my country is hard
more for them than for me
they hold their armour close
expecting me to blow them arrows
with curare. They don't expect
how much I'm hungry for news
they used to know; in their memories they carry
the freedom to skim rapids, trek
rainforest trails, climb mountains
photograph savannahs and waterfalls
walk the streets fearless in the days
before bandits and bodyguards, catch a taxi
safe in the knowledge there will be
no ambush, reach their destination safe
climb out of car doors with bold
white legs only susceptible to mosquitoes.
Those who came with bibles know
Forgive them Father for they know not what they do
and I for one just long to know
how it felt,
to walk the ceilings of my country
like Spiderman, and vault one country
to another, whilst Anansi still
sweet-talking, hoping to make a living
out of words.

Sixty Shades

That woman bundling all three copies
of *Sixty Shades* into her trolley
sideways up the Quaker Oats
the Chardonnay, the Three for £10 meat
the dog food and the bread
and at the checkout baling them out
with an expressionless face
paying with her credit card all business-like–
what will she unpack first
stack the food, hide the books
like chocolate in a secret place
where Mr Husband and the kids
don't go?
Or maybe she's alone, just her and doggy
loneliness bestowed through no fault
and yearning as we all do yearn
for something, anything to stoke the flame
feel the burn even for a moment
and the even sweeter moment of the falling.

Hawk

     swoops in for the kill
topaz eyes sharp
to the flicker of movement
the scent of blood, the pulse.

Early morning sacrifice
naked on blue tarpaulin
plucked out of cardboard boxes
the backs of cars.

Oilskin slick with dew
she cuts into the Carmarthen crowd
drawn to blue embroidery boxes
warming pans, Beswick china.

Later she'll regurgitate her prey
negotiate her mark-up
to wolves, ferrets, owls.

I Had a Lover Once

I had a lover once
who might have liked to be Roman
either that or he saw too many Metro- Goldwyn Meyer
flicks where dancing girls
fetched trays of delicacies to men who sat at tables
drinking out of chalices of brass.
What might have imprinted was
those lovelies laying about on sedans or bathing pools
who used their bellies as a platter filled with grapes
and cubes of Tuscan melons whilst the senile
had a natter and carried on with planning their campaigns.
What's different is the laughs we had
with grapes and cherries sliding off my belly
with me thinking what a waste
I should have saved the whipped cream for
the jelly and what with the doorbell and the dog
 making a mockers of us trying to be erotic
called it a day and settled for the chocolate.

When The Waters Came

They said that alligators crawled out of the mud; they were
hyper, really wild
talk about tails whipping and baring of teeth! At least one child
was barely whisked away in time, his legs dangling like string
behind
his father's Olympic stride.

The women didn't have time to do their hair, pick up a
hairbrush even
and that's saying some, these are land mermaids remember,
manatees,
lounge on back-steps when the cooking's done with brush and
comb,
dousing their hair with coconut oil, laughing at any men who
dared to
pluck a guitar string
believing themselves a dude.

The water ushered in the strangest things; Rupi's underwear
was caught high in a mango tree, waving strips of tangerine for
weeks to come;
her husband didn't know where to put his face.
They caught one creature, poor misunderstood thing,
all out of sorts, had lost both house and home
and he was swallowing everything, even a mobile phone
that rung and rung until the battery died,
and many wondered if the owner was still inside.

I Wanted To Raise Them Wild

I wanted to raise them wild
like oxblood daisies or fox cubs
faces turned up to the sun
or following scents moon-lit
and lemur-sprinkled
with an instinct for navigation
and languages unburdened by words.
They had danced even before birth
swimming in equatorial waters
earthed in tune
to the way things worked
and when their warm bodies left mine
they constantly returned;
you could see how quickly they learnt to walk.

But wildness was not to be, the greater plan
is to set them in rows like wheat, where their heads
may roll with the wind, feet tied to a ground
sterilised like hedgerows, cloned
in nurseries of sameness where even now
Aunties are marking their progress
ready to cut them down if they tread too far.
All I can do is hope that somewhere
a fox cub barking will serve to remind them
of the scent of bark, the passage of stars.

Between That River and This Sea

I read somewhere that sounds never actually disappear,
just relocate;
so that call, on a borrowed Bakelite phone, 1968
teenage voices floating still -

between that river and this sea
are forty-four years, two photographs
and a thousand letters
I never wrote lost within all the poems
I ever wrote,

(though one or two might have found their way via BWIA).

The photographs slotted still
in a yellow *Chu's Bookstore* plastic bag
Ice-Creams available here:
Main Street, New Amsterdam.

Surreal, this between-then-and-now,
punctuated by marriages, births and deaths,
babies' first steps, an orgasm or three
Papa Doc, 9/11...

The email now –
an old friend writes – he wants your phone number –
and between that river and this sea
a telephone call makes its cyber journey back to me
and an aging man is dreaming
of my virginity.

Names are Such Precious Things

Names are such precious things:
Morning Glory, now, that's a one
coming from prayer, that communion
with the soul, the world, some sun god.
You almost expect to see Cat Stevens
on the patio singing about the breaking of mornings
in ecstatic praise where an offering of such
an other-worldly blue comes tumbling
over the trellis
like the hair of our uncomplicated youth.

Before You Left For the Coast

... you returned my letters to me
a great wad weighed down in your arms like shopping.
Your shoes were shone
your hair smoothed
your eagerness to leave as brazen as a balloon

I did not hold you with my gaze
did not remind you with the uncrossing of my thighs
but offered you instead the smile reserved for goodbyes
a cheery wave, bright eyes.

I Always Went for The Wild Ones

I always went for the wild ones
Jimmy Cliff v Cat
Oh Baby Baby it's a wild world ...
Ain't no mp3 or cds can replace a 45
where me and Gail are curled up in my teenage bedroom
spinning discs like there's no tomorrow.
I've no idea how *Tracks of my Tears*
have made it till now Wales, 2013 (cyber date!)
Mr Smokey still cooking the chill
on a retro record player bought off the catalogue.
He's singing his heart out like Cat
while some old broad is adding the crackling
alongside the record-player
and the only wilderness is the woods running
outside, back 'o yard.

Them Go Walk Bush

Them go walk bush
That what them say back home
when lovely-doveyness gwine on
and people holding hand and thing
like them boyfren and girlfren
strolling the Botanic Gardens
laughing quiet and leaning up
behind palm tree. Only
Lawd when we find out the true reality
how that loving thing depend
on holding the man lolee
Lawd me mother bust my ass bad
for repeating nasty things Daphne
next door tell me;
and after licks
and me mouth wash out
with soap
is three Our Fathers
and twenty Hail Marys is punish they punish me.

My Ears are Naked, Waiting

My ears are naked, waiting
the column of my throat pulsating
breathless with desire
unadorned

They should be illuminated,
draped in filigree of silver
I, an Empress
Doyen of diamonds, Diva
of diamante and gold
intergalactic courtesan
whose eyes rise from a galaxy of night
to roam a minutiae of stars
moon stops of blue
a flight deck of sapphires
iced against my skin

A smouldering throat lifts
in abeyance,
both host and hostess
my ears are naked, waiting;
a sacrifice to light.

As a Full-grown Woman

As a full-grown woman and new
to this country I could never see
the need for screwing in the open.
No I'm not talking dogging,
that word had not yet been invented.
No; this simple English desire to commune
with nature, find bliss in haystacks
and fields of oats. I began to view
white men warily, not understanding
the thrill of corn stalks up your butt
or cowflies resting on your thighs after a visit
from a steamy pile.
We who grew up with sand-flies
and yellow-fever mosquitoes have a penchant
for clean sheets and hotel rooms
and true I should have held fast to this
then that farmer wouldn't have chased us
off his corn.

Small Thumbs

Small thumbs push chalk on slate
Forging *A for Apple*
Knowing only red DC apples at Christmas
And mangoes and tamarind balls
But under the heat of a convent roof
Sloping with nuns and wild canes
What stirs is the shape of *A*
Scratched time and time again
Rubbed out with a chalky arm
Until it slants just right
An *A* with a curl and a loop
Until perfection and time
To move on to *Bs*, *Cs*, and so many others
Where they all waited
Like friends asking you to come on out to play.

Flowers

She hated flowers, bunch of tarts
tufty heads and stupid faces
reaching for the sun.
She hated the way they dressed to kill
dazzling with colour luring you
to draw their noxious scent near.
She hated the way they lay
on the draining board whilst you ran
around in a ritual collecting vases and water
sighing with the resignation of virgins.
She hated the way they were offered by liars
stinking of drink and late home
and how easy they were to reach for
the sick and the dying.
She hated the way they watch you go about
your business, their petals on the table
falling like tears reminding her
just a couple more days they are outa here
and mighta stayed around longer
if she'd watered them.
And she hated the way they leaned
on garden walls or lamp-posts
in sheaths of plastic fading from a nest
of cellophane that will never decompose
and screamed that silent scream
of utterance.
But most of all, most of all
she hated the way they try, to take the place of words.

That Scene in *True Blood*

That scene in *True Blood, Series 1, Episode 2*:
and they're standing under a thin moon
skin white with flickering flashes of blue
the vampire, saturnine with the Heathcliff brood
and *her*, blonde hair upswept, transfixed
as he asks her to remove her clip
that symbol of resistance

That pale white neck with the one raised vein
waiting like a rabbit freeze-framed
limbs still, heart flipped, eyes locked
considering the moment;
considering the moment when his bat-face falls
like the shadows of night in her pool-blue eyes
of fright

... and honey, you are fourteen years old again
necking on the darkened porch, door closed
against your Momma sleeping under
the mosquito net, the crucifix rising
on her Portuguese throat in the lift
and fall of her breathing. Your true
blood pounds September tide

a daughter transformed into a thing of the night
flesh open for the Annunciation.
And the loverman's tongue is smooth and wild
with the rich deep scent
of the honeysuckle vine

and the time-line shifts
with the night-hawk's fall
and momma eye flickers
and the crucifix shooting a sunrise wide
blow the girl-child
straight outa the kingdom

Perhaps
(for Steven)

Just before dying I'll rest my last sigh on your upturned palm
There, in that dip, it will nestle like a small bird

With one tiny eye fastened on your face
Remembering my secret observances –

That voice that first captured me
The smile that turned me to liquid

The way I fitted into your arms.

I'll remember too that you never said *no*,
Always *yes*, or *perhaps*, even as a frown cut into your brow.

And after dying? Who knows?
Just run your thumb into the cove of your palm,

Perhaps you'll feel that lift of cool air,
A tiny flicker, me.

Letter from Kong to Anna

Dearest Anna,
So here we are again, 2005, and nothing's changed.
The word on the street still –
Beauty killed the Beast.
This time they wrote a sunset *and*
an ice-rink into the screenplay
but guess what –
you're still teaching *me* how to speak.
This 05 remake is more slick, yeah,
the air thick with monsters
displaying all the savagery that celluloid
and talons can convey -
(you wait, that CGI will be something
I tell you),
but here we go - the hero lives
to fight another day
 and through the underbelly
crawls the thick-lipped and the tom-tom
and the dance. *Maann ...*
it's the heart of darkness beating
in Manhattan and in Central Park.
Y'know honey, I guess I'm the subject
of a thousand third-year studies
Media, Sexuality, Gender, Race...
me the Beast, a throwback
beyond even Fay, to that high old time
with trees, silver-backed gorilla
on his knees, cradling vocally challenged
blonde in fist. Believe me Babe,

any guy would play the game
for a one-way ticket to the great
US of A.
But let's treasure these moments Anna,
let them capture us soft-focused and serene
freeze-frame this New York skyscrape;
for below us (*shush darling, miles!*)
just who's roaming the sidewalk
willing Miss America to scream? Hey?
x KK

Oh Mr Cohen

(For Chantal Lammertyn)

Oh Mr Cohen -!
we could have had such a fine time if we stepped out
me on your arm like a geisha
the words around us dancing like monarch butterflies
you looking sharp with the hat and your neat step
over the puddles; stopping to contemplate the weight
of the soul in water and how love can rise
like a bubble and sink like a stone.
The perfect phrase hangs just out of reach –
a baby's foot so soft we stroke its' sole and toes
like cherries pulled into our mouths with the juices streaming
but oh what a baptism over our nice clothes!
Our friends will love us anyroad,
waving from the party with cigarettes and wine,
their articulate fingers –
Neruda and Walcott, Chantal Lammertyn ...
And my heart is bursting with happiness
as all the time the conversation
flows I'm alive and Chantal did not break her neck
down the well but is writing to me still –
My little firefly, my Caribbean songbird –
and from this cold white tomb where I assemble these notes
Lorca peels himself from the walls and says
It's worth the sacrifice. It's worth the sacrifice.

Seeds

With my face into the pillow I feel you burst
inside me
like a watermelon
split
by the face of the sun

words are strangled by cotton
shower, cascade, waterfall, rain
seeds swim upstream
through every rivulet, ripple, contraction
spasm of muscle
thigh tidal channel
O God O God O God

they are entering each fissure
each crevice, each cell
they are singing war songs as they swim
songs of home and country
motherlands and fatherlands
there are no orphans here
no adoptees
this is *their* country
me.

O Woman

And perhaps now is the time to tell
that hard-faced women don't put the look on their face
life does, or more to the point
a half life: half-full, half- empty whatever.
It's uncomfortable to think of aging women
still waiting with their face to the window
ear to the sound of the door or the telephone;
hard to stir any empathy for a body slowed,
nose amongst the nasturtiums pulling weeds
or inhaling its deep scent conscious of her knees
on the ground as if in prayer but longing for
some Dionysius or Apollo even a minotaur
to approach her from behind and nudge their woolly heads
into that soft space the back of her neck.
We'd prefer to think of Cameron Diaz
whose perfect skin the camera and our eyes love to linger on
easy to transfer all our desires and feel so right that love
and beauty beat the shared coupled heart in tune. And I
wouldn't know where to start chronicling all the wasted desire
like bubbles from champagne or a chocolate fountain
just pouring itself away for nothing.
Hey, Mister Spanish guy, do you remember that woman
in her garden after the school run stretching her body
out on the lawn?
She knew you were there
hanging from next door's window, dictionary in hand.
And Hey Mr young German, how her lips burned
with the wanting to pull on your freedom to walk
mountains while her children

bound her like a washing line wild with a Southern wind.
And I couldn't begin to note the frenzy the sun brought
guys like Gods at a music festival, Bacchus in denim blue
the hairs on his legs bleached blonde and all she wanted
was to fuck him face down on a bale of straw with Neil Young
singing *Heart of Gold*.
O woman,
you walked the tightrope so neatly between virgin and whore
and time eroding your body is so narcissistic, measuring evil
out like hormones, stealing some and leaving some so you're
still rushing rampant like a hare racing a timeless meadow
and only the gravity of mind forcing her down to the ground
pinning her down like a doe.

Far Country
(For Eloise)

Your voice on the telephone
telling me your waters broke
and even as I stare out the window
in this far country I'm swimming to reach you
swimming as she is, our little Rose.
I can see her face folded still within your womb
hesitant to leave, safe in the world your body
built around her, a water-world
of muted colour and lullabies sung through skin
sailing like a schooner through oceans.
The hum of docksides and ports is waiting to lure her;
she has been sea-horse and porpoise, a passenger
on a container ship, an umbilical cargo
and you a mermaid, half fish, half woman
pulled by the moon and the tides.
And so we wait, each paused for the turn
beached for the moment she slips from her aquatic world
and comes to walk between us.

The Feminine

I for one, always appreciated doors opened for me
seats vacated, and to be bought lunch.
My equality in this marketplace never depended
on the demise of gentlemen.
We who never had to tie ourselves to railings
inherited a limitless horizon.
The feminine is fathomless and powerful as oceans
holding moons and minds,
provoking wars simply with the terror of its beauty.
Remember this, young sisters, when your harridan mouths
gob and roar and scream your independence
in city streets, fuelled by the light in some guys eyes
and a short night.
Listen to the blood pump in your ears, as he sleeps.

If I'd Been a Mathematician

If I'd been a mathematician, what sum over the years
all those hours of longing for lovers
who may or may not come calling ...?
Inestimable hours, knitting desolation into a shield
that refused to migrate from its fragile nest
in the breast of Victorian poetry.

A geologist even, who else to chart the terrain
of a disconsolate heart against a landscape
scarped from tale and legend –
sirens, lorelies, maidens waiting
by castellated windows for a hero
to mount summits, blaze deserts
unlock the front door...

O but, maybe the world needed to evolve; for time
to offer a bird's eye view of the bleached hulls
of ships escarped in desert plains, or
archipelagos spewed across cerulean seas
from the throats of angry volcanoes
and all my letters, both written and un-written
tessellated prayer flags waving from Samarkand to Chicago

Ah – I would an astronomer be,
astrologers just fill your head with stars;
then this whole darn journey would have been informed
by gravity, instead of harbouring disparate images –
the soul weighted, a buoy on a limitless sea,
and dreams leaning like ladders
on endlessly diminishing spirals of suns.

And Darling

And darling, so much hope still invested
in waiting for the crunch of wheels on gravel
the clip of the latch on the gate
the falling sigh on the doormat
a mobile phone weighted in the palm
like prayer beads
you have no messages
you have no messages

Those Treacherous Hormones

It seems we never get the balance quite right
except at the beginning when all is chemistry and lust
eyes locking, touch electrified, the eyes' urge to drown
a metaphor perhaps for sperm swimming upstream
like salmon.

After the frenzy, the mid-stream position
expectation rising and falling like proving dough
Keep her hungry, promise Tuesday, call on Friday.
If he calls I'll be busy.

Who can recall that first moment love becomes a game
of chess?
Some lovers wait, concede to the hungry queen
whilst others measure out three-quarters of the heart
just leaving room to breathe;
and forever the fight will be
how much we expect and need
from the lungs of another being.

And is love better to give or receive
and if we really cherish the way he laughs
regardless of whether we're in the frame?

Those treacherous hormones only know one thing:
increase and multiply;
and they don't care how they do it
only that we continue the journey
a channel of stars in an infinite universe.

Four Sonnets for Four Almost Lovers

I

We were Dali's children, lavender fields
stretched through your window; Sarre Windmill turned
against a light sky. Your fingers revealed
each perfect page of your portfolio, burned
against tissue, paper, the phrase of my neck.
Your subjects waited, their limbs transformed
into branches, hair heavy as velvet
cloaking their bodies, vacuous, unborn.
Under no illusions I was a subject too,
young, hungry for the inflection of your
fingers against the canvas of my skin, new
to surrealism, a fledging, raw.
Desire, in my unaccustomed throat
subject shifting, lady crossing the moat.

II

If I passed you now I wouldn't know you
and I would be Invisible, the wrong
side of sixty, not skinny in denim blue
swinging on the front gate, a Hermits' song
juicy like a mango on my pearlised lips.
Portuguese boys: under altar-boy vestments
desire rose like incense, girls' hula hips
breaking the monopoly of sacraments.
It wasn't that you were agile or cute
knew stuff about cricket and the H-bomb
or lived in Queen Elizabeth Avenue;
it was you on my porch, a phenomenon
and me, conscious of the way I spoke
the strange pressure of words against my throat.

III

You were no Belafonte. Even as girls
Danced around you, your eyes were searching,
Your palms on the bongos skimming the waves
Reaching beyond Santana, listening.
Some boys fell my way like guavas, the flesh
Of their smiles studded with seeds, teeth like tomb
– stones, clean of names, light of History, enmeshed
In New York dreams and Top Twenty tunes.
But you drummer boy, retracing the rhythms
Of sail and bone, limb and chain, utterance
Broken mid-stream, praise-songs of Africans
Not yet celebrated, refused that dance.
Like ships we passed, migrating birds who knew
Our journey was bigger than me, or you.

IV

You may be some fat professor now, bald
At a functional desk in some smart uni
Cologne, maybe Bremen; still enthralled
With life, cute wife, kids and Philosophy.
But there's the young you in my living-room
Fit and lean from walking the Cornish coast
And I'm your landlady, kids, partner, broom
Drawn to your sweet mouth and smooth throat.
We argue ardently on Art, Kant, Jung
While I stir spaghetti on the stove
And *No Woman no Cry* is being sung
By Bob Marley on the radio.
And oh the longing! And that small step
That stolen kiss on your naked, naked lips...

xxx

Willie Gunboat

That Canadian reading poetry in the Carmarthen bar
Long blond hair and blue eyes ...
It could have been Willie Gunboat
(yes really), another white man abroad
in 1969; sun-burnt knees straddling a borrowed Raleigh
circling a West Indian street, sexy Mr Teach.
There he is in Chu's Ice-Cream parlour
Surrounded by teenagers eager to please
Drop the *Sir*, accept a strawberry milkshake.
Skinny me, leaning in the presence of a real hippie
Bring him home to mum, also in the glaze of a white
Man's smile, never mind he's 25 and me 15. Just look
At that long hair swinging down his back and the twinkly
Blue eyes of the conqueror. And I'm so hot for him
From the minute he plays The Boxtops' 'The Letter'
He and his guitar under the Headmaster's office.
So off to the movies we go (yes really) and he's almost
My SBF until one of us pulls the brakes and my errant eye
Rests lightly on a home-boy.
So here we are in Carmarthen and there sit
Those laughing girls and this old fool
Sipping tea in a corner reminiscing some long ago shit
When crikey, even their mothers were not even born.

Take Me By This Open Window

Take me by this open window here
where the sea crashes on the rocks
angry at its own surge
and the land laughing
a drawbridge
above

I want to feel that power in the prison
of your arms, fusing me between
these shutters and you
the salt spray from the reef
on your
tongue

Here I can wake from nightmares of falling
empty as an echo floating
on wild cliffs in the wind
here I taste my own blood
on my lips, lift my throat
for the slice of your mouth

Take me by this open window
here, where the sea cuts the rock
catch me as I fall
quiet as a ripple
high on your chest like a sweat-drop
catch me, at that moment of sinking

My Daughter is Writing Me Letters

My daughter is writing me letters
They arrive and fall on the doormat
My name and address rising like scattered birds

And I remember the pages of exercise books
English homework flying feathers and spines
Across the living room
Her elbows and face on the kitchen table
The broken pencil in her fist

Now I don't care what she writes
Only that she writes
Vowels and consonants
Are cradled waiting for the slit
Of my fingers where heart meets heart
And communication stirs itself awake
Through the calligraphy of reason

The envelope sits in my palm
Like a nugget of gold

O Spirits

Let me rock then, in the cradle of my imaginings -
Lift my face like a child
Like a young wolf to the moon
My throat full of gospel songs

Let my cheeks be as soft as turned earth
My lips bruised as plums
Let me trace each brook to its source
Each step back to the slums.

Gods have dwelled here
Roamed with the full force of battle
Sent their messengers before them
In an array of disguises

Primeval, battle-worn, whistling
Through trees and stone, Old Testament
To the bone:
Lilith dancing like Isadora, Isis a disco diva
Mary with her pained son.
Theresa, Bernadette, all perched on my altar
Amongst the mascara and the rosary;
Even an emissary from the East
Held fast in my kohl-rimmed eyes and blue laugh.

Incantations tumbled like corn
Its music borne on beads and trembling
In Hallelujahs, Hare Khrisnas, Oms.

Then Reason and Enlightenment,
Descartes, Kant, Darwin, Mill
and from the West of Africa, the drum.

Oh spirits, leave me be.

We Would Never, We Said

We would never, we said, get like that
Our glances briefly resting on that couple, sixty-plus
Staring into the fire
His fingers curled round half a mild
Hers travelling intermittently from the G&T
To stroke the collie on the floor.
Not a word passed between them.

Your hands slid up my skirt
And my eyes lingered on your mouth
As Adam and the Ants rumbled from the jukebox
Someone shouted for twenty B & H, and the smell of the sea
Blew in each time a punter tumbled in or out.

I was laughing at your joke
On my way to the loo
And caught her eye, sure I heard her say
'Make it last girlie, it *will* happen to you.'

The Moaning Poem

Let's get it over in a single poem, a jolly good British moan
on the random basketing of all our eggs
exchanging city life for a pile of Welsh stones
whose only credibility is a garden wild and beautiful
with slugs black and fat as tyres.

One small pebble can easily become a landslide
as easily as 'state' neatly rhymes with 'grate'
and that's us, the hunter-gatherers rooting
for firewood at Llanstephan, and wandering Tescos
with a tenner in hand. Whilst we're about it
let's mention the unpaid phone, the cost
of keeping in touch, my hours of loneliness
the erratic internet, the oil-tank empty
the cold of a caustic winter.

Such is the lot of party girls who too late
decide to become land girls entering a war-zone
entirely of their making, then waste their tears
remembering the length of time it takes
to set roots in new earth
the scalding shame of becoming a statistic.
Enough? Enough.

The Sun is Visiting Today

The sun is visiting today
And I go to greet him in the garden
Where communion is easy and instant.
No lover can stroke me as he does
None can make me whistle
Or oil my limbs in that slow Caribbean way.
In discourse over the lilies
His promises bleed through the spears
Of hostas, reminding me not of canefields
But Broadstairs, and children growing like stalks
Through festivals inhabited by dragons, their bodies
Studded with sand. Finite moments
Dogged by time's swift passage.
Sometimes I wonder whether our re-unions
Would have meant any more if I'd been born
Norwegian, or Inuit. I doubt it.

Would that I had been a Martha Gellhorn

Would that I had been a Martha Gellhorn, or Isadora;
a Rainbow Warrior, or foot soldier for Compassion
For World Farming. Would that I had taken the story
of lost peoples to the UN and secured a treaty for
permanent peace and liberty. Would that I had un-schooled
my daughters from hours of pre-ordained shite
and rode our bikes across San Salvador and seen
the sun rise on Galapagos.
I should have gone to Greenham, built rafts
for peace, marched on Whitehall, instead
of playing homage to imagined roots and learning
Ghanain dance believing I was some griot
whose words were gentle weapons of persuasion.
Yeah right. Everybody's shouting now and still
girl children are having their genitalia sliced
with razors and rusty knives
in villages I may have cycled through
my children's heads blazing against a horizon of blue.

Dylan is Playing the Djembe

Dylan is playing the djembe
nine o'clock of an evening filled with the memory
of sand and showers, rocks and seals
and the mystery of no whales in Wales.
He may remember this moment
although he's only three:
Granny's cottage
the smooth texture of goatskin
under his small palms
the giggling of sisters snuggling down
Kanisia sending mobile messages
back to the boyfriend in Somerset.
In Sandgate his cousin tribe watch dvds
jump trampolines; Chloe at sixteen all grown up
preparing for college.

This djembe has travelled from Africa
played at festivals, accompanied poetry;
now it cuts discordant rhythms into a new night
rhythm experimental but sonic as his name.

Someday he may make the link
or find it here, buried within this poem, Summer, Wales, 2013.

Me and Eliza Carthy

Me and Eliza Carthy are singing in tune
Cutting the stale air of a Friday afternoon
Where seven days of lonesome
Have cut me through and through.

The woman in the mirror looks
Nothing at all like me, singing as she cooks
And dancing with the curtains closed
In the African dress I bought from Pancho's store.

Somewhere the man I love is driving
Along another hopeless road.
He's hoping I'll be waiting with a smile so full
Of loving with my eyes alive and pumping

But it ain't gonna happen so
It ain't gonna happen so.

The journey through the music
Has moved right off the highway
Travelling down those rutted roads
Where only women walk

They're worn down with all the walking
'Cos all they want to do is dance
And sing and that's why
Their eyes will look right past him
And out the open door.

Me and Eliza Carthy are singing in tune

Me and Eliza Carthy are singing in tune.
On a Friday afternoon.

The Season of Hands

In order to know this earth my feet walked it;
Wye to Chilham, with women who knew the way
their wisdom ranging
from exocets to names of flowers
growing wild and the cries of birds from the hedgerow.

So here now, I dry my tears
in memory of coffee bars and friends, some dead,
some living still in another life. Where once the sea
had parted me from all I knew and loved,
this time it is the land.

It is the earth running beneath the Severn,
turning away from me
in my small patch of wilderness, refusing to be named
sending brambles sharp as barbed wire and nettles coarse
as market women, to bleed me to the bone.

I wanted my father then to smoke out
the marabunta nest from underneath my window.
But this year, this year,
my hands have come to know this earth
bound as we all are in histories of massacre.

The messages between us borne on the slow hum
of bees, the swallow that didn't return
the red kite circling. I know
that beneath us our lungs are in turmoil

as harsh blades wrench the limbs of rainforests kicking in a
silent scream as the seas are scraped dry with drift nets,
as women's faces shrivel under acid
and girls lie helpless beneath the butchers' hands.

I fear for young men under the guidance of evil,
their innocent minds
warped,
their love for women
gnarled as the twisted roots of mangroves.

Messages tear me through and through, thrusting
my soul inwards, my senses reliving the memories
of innocence and quick bursts of youthful passion.

For each thing a season;
here is my season of hands: learning to read
the destiny of compost and flint,
my body tuned
to dawn, rising to nurture what is cradled here,

watch the earth unfold its gifts:
yellow courgettes blazing in a lily-boat of leaves
clematis ruby rich against a white wall
and the sun, glorious this summer,
bringing the memories of mangoes

but offering me a host of butterflies
who re-interpret my words
in the light of the wasps' sting. Here
let me rest in a semblance of paradise
with all the beauty and fear that it brings.